Manners with a Library Book

Way to Be!

by Amanda Doering Tourville   illustrated by Chris Lensch

PICTURE WINDOW BOOKS
Minneapolis, Minnesota

Special thanks to our advisers for their expertise:

Kay A. Augustine, Ed.S.
National Character Development Consultant and Trainer
West Des Moines, Iowa

Terry Flaherty, Ph.D., Professor of English
Minnesota State University, Mankato

Editor: Shelly Lyons
Designer: Tracy Davies
Page Production: Melissa Kes
Art Director: Nathan Gassman
Editorial Director: Nick Healy
The illustrations in this book were created digitally.

Picture Window Books
1710 Roe Crest Drive
North Mankato, MN 56003
www.capstonepub.com

Library of Congress Cataloging-in-Publication Data
Tourville, Amanda Doering, 1980-
Manners with a library book / by Amanda Doering Tourville ; illustrated by
Chris Lensch.
p. cm. — (Way to Be! Manners)
Includes bibliographical references and index.
ISBN: 978-1-4048-5314-0 (library binding)
ISBN: 978-1-4048-5315-7 (paperback)
1. Library etiquette—Juvenile literature. 2. Etiquette for children and
teenagers—Juvenile literature. 3. Books—Mutilation, defacement, etc.—
Prevention—Juvenile literature. I. Lensch, Chris, ill. II. Title.
 Z716.43.T68 2009
395.5'3—dc22   2008039134

Printed in the United States   6069

The library is a great place to check out books. It is important to use good manners with a library book. Good manners allow others to enjoy the book when you are done.

There are lots of ways to use good manners with a library book.

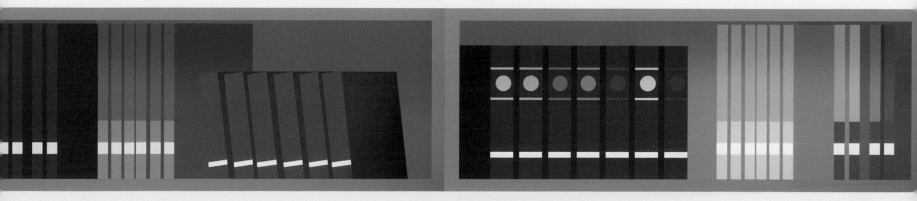

Tia and her brother Jaden each find two books at the library. They follow the library's instructions for checking out books.

They are using good manners.

Back at home, it's time for a snack. Tia and Jaden don't eat or drink while reading their books. They put away the books and then have a snack.

They are using good manners.

Snack time is over. Tia and Jaden are excited to read. They wash and dry their hands before touching the books.

They are using good manners.

9

Tia reads to her younger sister. She keeps the book out of her sister's reach. Tia makes sure her sister doesn't rip or stain any of the pages.

Tia is using good manners.

Jaden carefully turns each page of the library book. He doesn't want to tear any of them.

He is using good manners.

Jaden never folds the corner of a page.
He always uses a bookmark to hold his place.

He is using good manners.

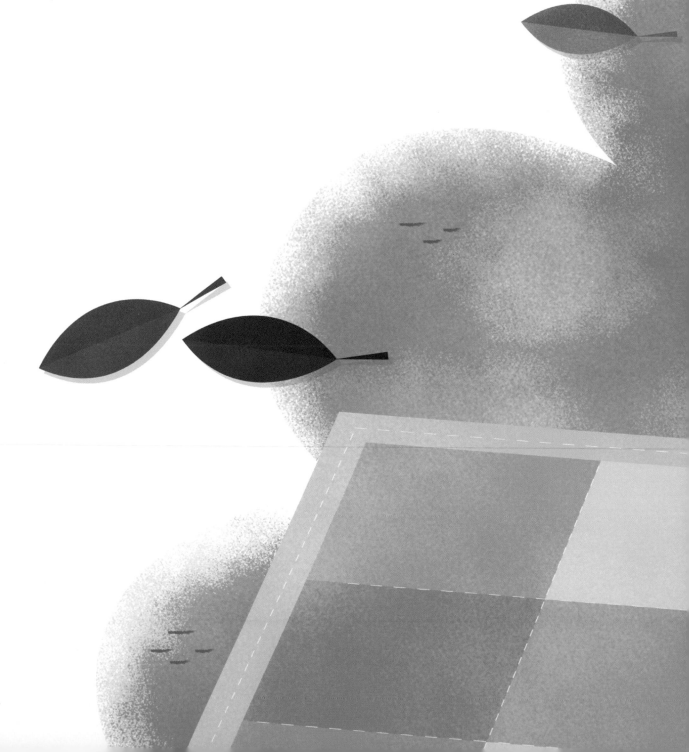

Tia and Jaden keep their library books in bags.
They make sure their pets can't reach the books.

They are using good manners.

Tia's books are due, but she's not done reading them yet. She goes to the library to renew the books.

She is using good manners.

Jaden's books are due back today, too. He returns them on time by putting them in the book bin.

He is using good manners.

It is important to use good manners with a library book. When you take care of library books, the books last a long time. Many people in your community will have a chance to read them.

Fun Facts

The world's largest library is the Library of Congress in Washington, D.C.

The Library of Congress contains materials in about 470 languages.

What is believed to be the world's first library was opened around 283 B.C. in Alexandria, Egypt.

There are more than 123,000 libraries in the United States.

The first book ever made using a printing press was made in Germany in 1456.

People from all over the world can now read many books online.

To Learn More

More Books to Read

DeGezelle, Terri. *Manners at the Library*. Mankato, Minn.: Capstone Press, 2005.

Finn, Carrie. *Manners in the Library*. Minneapolis: Picture Window Books, 2007.

Leaf, Munro. *Manners Can Be Fun*. New York: Universe Pub., 2004.

Thomas, Pat. *My Manners Matter: A First Look at Being Polite*. New York: Barron's, 2006.

On the Web

FactHound offers a safe, fun way to find educator-approved Internet sites related to this book.

Here's what you do:
1. Visit www.facthound.com
2. Choose your grade level.
3. Begin your search.

This book's ID number is 9781404853140

Look for all of the books in the Way to Be! Manners series:

Manners at a Friend's House

Manners at School

Manners at the Table

Manners in Public

Manners in the Library

Manners in the Lunchroom

Manners on the Playground

Manners on the School Bus

Manners on the Telephone

Manners with a Library Book

Index

following library instructions, 4

keeping books out of reach, 10, 16

keeping food away from books, 6

renewing books, 18

returning books, 20

turning pages carefully, 13

using a bookmark, 14

using book bags, 16

washing hands, 9

24